PEACE & WAR

by

Charlie Ogden

©2017
Book Life
King's Lynn
Norfolk PE30 4LS

ISBN: 978-1-78637-141-6

Written by:
Charlie Ogden

Edited by:
Grace Jones

Designed by:
Natalie Carr

CONTENTS

Words in **bold** can be found in the glossary on page 31.

PEACE AND WAR

Peace and war are two very important **issues** in today's world and they are often discussed in the media. People regularly talk about how terrible war is and how we should all try to make the world a more peaceful place. The reason that these two issues are often talked about together is because they are very closely linked.

'Peace' is sometimes a difficult word to define. Peace can be thought of as a state of **tranquillity**, where people are happy and everyone gets along with each other. Many people believe that peace is the most important thing to aim for because it is the only way that everyone can be happy. Other people, however, view peace as always being linked to war. For these people, peace is simply a time when there is no war or violence.

'MEDIA' IS THE COLLECTIVE NAME FOR ALL OF THE POPULAR FORMS OF COMMUNICATION, SUCH AS TELEVISION, RADIO, NEWSPAPERS AND THE INTERNET.

These symbols are known around the world as signs of peace.

War is usually described as **conflict**, violence and fighting between separate and organised groups of people. Each side in a war will usually have their own **military**, weapons, leaders, soldiers, **tactics** and reasons for fighting. And, of course, war always leads to loss of life, injured **civilians**, people being forced out of their homes and cities and towns being destroyed.

THE ACTIVITIES INVOLVED IN FIGHTING A WAR ARE CALLED 'WARFARE'.

Just from these short explanations of what peace and war are, it is easy to see that living in a peaceful world would be a lot better than living in a world where wars are always being fought. Fewer soldiers die in wars today than in almost any other period of history, so many people believe that we are getting closer and closer to world peace. However, there is still a very long way to go.

The reason that so many people talk about and work towards making the world a more peaceful place is because, for the first time in history, world peace might actually be possible. Humans have come a long way in the last 100 years and we have more knowledge and technology now than ever before in history.

For almost all of human history, wars have been fought over resources and supplies. Resources and supplies are things that people need in order to survive – they include things such as food, water, money, energy and land. However, wars fought over resources and supplies could soon become a thing of the past.

One in every nine people – about 795 million people worldwide – don't always have enough food to eat. In 2015, however, enough food was produced to feed the entire population of the world twice over and in today's world we have the technology to transport food to almost anywhere. With a little help from everyone, we could soon live in a world where everyone has enough food to eat.

Other reasons for going to war are harder to prevent. One of the most common reasons for going to war throughout history has been to gain power. Civilians have gone to war against their own **governments** in order to gain power over their country. Governments have gone to war because they want more power over their people. And leaders have gone to war simply because they want more power over the world.

Culture can also often lead to war. Different groups of people around the world often fall out with each other because they have different cultures. This may be because their cultures include different religions or because they hold different **values.**

Even though people around the world are becoming more **tolerant** and accepting, these reasons for going to war may never completely disappear because people are often motivated by power or their culture.

TYPES OF WAR

There are many different types of war. In the past, battles were often very similar – two armies would face each other and fight until one side **surrendered** or was completely killed. These battles would have been more likely to last hours than years and people would have fought using horses and swords rather than tanks, bombs and guns.

However, our wars have changed as our technology has improved, meaning that we can now fight wars on the other side of the world while using all sorts of weapons. Because of this, there are now lots of different types of war. The different types of war are based on where the fighting takes place, who is fighting whom and who has paid for the weapons, **ammunition** and supplies.

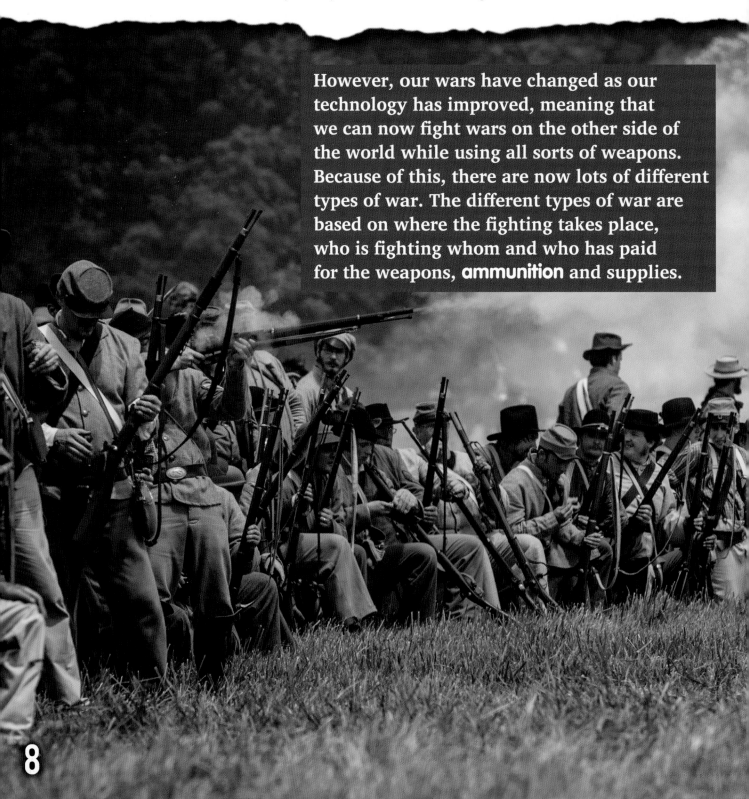

One of the most common types of war today, as well as throughout history, are civil wars. Civil wars are wars that are fought between two groups of people from the same country. Civil wars occur for three main reasons:

TO TAKE CONTROL OVER AN ENTIRE COUNTRY

The English Civil War that took place between 1642 and 1651 is an example of this type of civil war. The Roundheads wanted England to be controlled by a government, whereas the Royalists wanted the country to be controlled by a king or queen.

TO BECOME AN INDEPENDENT COUNTRY

The Second Sudanese War that took place between 1983 and 2005 is an example of this type of civil war. It resulted in South Sudan becoming an **independent** country away from Sudan.

TO GET RID OF A GOVERNMENT

The Libyan Civil War that took place in 2011 is an example of this type of civil war. The war ended when the government was finally removed from power in October of 2011.

GUERRILLA WARS

Rather than gathering a large army together in one place and then attacking the enemy, guerrilla wars use lots of small groups of soldiers who can more easily move around. Guerrilla warfare is often used in places where the **terrain** makes it difficult for large armies to move around, like in jungles or on mountains.

Guerrilla warfare uses the terrain to make it easier to attack large groups of enemies. One of the most common ways that this is done is through ambushes. An ambush is where a group hides, often in jungle or on the side of a mountain, and waits for their enemy to come close enough before launching a surprise attack. In successful ambushes, groups of only 10 or 20 people can easily defeat hundreds of enemies.

PROXY WARS

Proxy wars are wars where one side attempts to hurt their enemy by costing them money and attacking their **allies**. Proxy wars usually start when two powerful countries are at war, but they don't want to fight each other directly because it would cause too much damage and cost too much money. So, instead of fighting each other directly, one country might start fighting the other country's allies.

North Korea

South Korea

Korean War **memorial**, Washington, D.C.

This was the case in the Korean War that took place between 1950 and 1953. At the time, the United States of America (U.S.A.) was at war with Russia. Instead of fighting each other directly, they fought each other through the Korean War. The U.S.A. sent soldiers, money and weapons to South Korea, whereas Russia sent money, supplies and weapons to North Korea. Although the war cost both the U.S.A. and Russia a lot of money, many people believe that a lot more people would have died if the two powerful countries had fought each other directly.

CONSEQUENCES OF WAR

It is well-known that the **consequences** of war can be frightening and terrible.

A huge number of soldiers have died while fighting in battle. Since the start of the 20th century, it has been possible for wars to kill thousands of people in just one day.

THE BATTLE OF THE SOMME IN WORLD WAR I LEFT NEARLY 60,000 BRITISH SOLDIERS DEAD OR INJURED AFTER JUST ONE DAY.

On top of this, many cities and towns are also destroyed during wars. This has also become easier to do in recent years, as better technology has led to bigger and more powerful bombs being created.

Wars also cost huge amounts of money, meaning that fighting a long war can leave a country very poor. However, there are other consequences of war that should also be talked about.

REFUGEES

Wars can often lead to a lot of people becoming refugees. Refugees are people who are forced to leave their country because they are scared that they will get attacked or killed. Being a refugee is very scary as you can't go back to your home and you don't know if you will be able to find a safe place to live in another country.

The South Sudanese Civil War, which started in 2013, has forced over 700,000 people to leave their homes in South Sudan and move to nearby countries.

Because of the powerful weapons that are used in modern wars, it is very common for countries at war to become dangerous places to live. Cities are often bombed, which leads to homes being destroyed and families having nowhere to live. On top of this, wars that start because of some cultural conflict can lead to people being attacked because of their **race** or religion. These two things mean that modern wars that are based around cultural differences often lead to many people becoming refugees.

INTERNATIONAL LAW

While each country has their own set of laws, there are also international laws. International laws are agreements between different countries and they are often related to **human rights**, the environment and trading supplies and resources. International laws are often called 'treaties' or 'conventions'.

THIS MAP SHOWS ALL OF THE COUNTRIES THAT ARE IN NATO – THE NORTH ATLANTIC TREATY ORGANIZATION. THE 28 COUNTRIES IN NATO HAVE ALL SIGNED A PEACE TREATY THAT SAYS THAT THEY WILL NOT FIGHT EACH OTHER AND THAT THEY WILL HELP TO PROTECT EACH OTHER IN ANY FUTURE WARS.

However, lots of international laws are also concerned with peace and war. When wars come to an end, peace treaties are sometimes created. Peace treaties are a type of international law and they explain how the countries involved in a war will work together now that the war has come to an end.

Other times when wars come to an end, international laws are made about what should be allowed in wars in the future. During World War I, lots of different poisonous gases were used by both sides. After the war, many people agreed that these gases were too terrible and that they weren't **humane**. Because of this, the Geneva Protocol was made in 1928, which made it illegal under international law to use poisonous gas during a war.

HUMAN LIFE

Soldiers aren't the only people who can lose their lives during a conflict. In many wars throughout history, lots of civilians have also been killed. Since the beginning of the 20th century, one of the most common ways that civilians have died during wars is from bombings.

Enemy cities are bombed during wars for many different reasons. Sometimes it is because there are factories there that make weapons and other times it is because there are large army bases there. Whenever cities are bombed, lots of civilians die.

During the Rwandan Civil War that took place in the 1990s, around 800,000 Rwandan civilians were killed because of their race. This **atrocity** is now known as the Rwandan genocide.

Rwanda

However, sometimes civilians are killed on purpose during a war because of their race or religion. When a group tries to kill every person who is part of a certain race or religion, no matter if they are soldiers or civilians, it is called genocide. Many people see genocide as the worst thing that can happen during a war.

WARS THROUGHOUT HISTORY
AMERICAN WAR OF INDEPENDENCE

Before 1775, America and all of the people who lived there were considered to be part of Britain. However, people in America didn't like the British government because they were being asked to pay British **taxes**. Because of this, 13 of the **colonies** in America decided to fight the British in order to become an independent country. This way they could decide how their colonies were run as well as how much tax they should pay. In 1782, after many years of fighting, the British government accepted defeat and agreed that the U.S.A. was its own, independent country.

The 13 colonies formed the Continental Congress, which was a sort of government that was used to organise the fighting against the British. In July, 1776, the Continental Congress created and signed the Declaration of Independence, which explained how America would be governed once they won the war against the British.

Bayonet

Musket

Cannon

Muskets took a long time to reload, so many muskets had bayonets on them in case the enemy got too close.

Date: 1775 - 1783
Deaths: Around 8,500 soldiers
Countries Involved: Britain and America
Main Weapons: Muskets, bayonets and cannons

AMERICAN WAR IN AFGHANISTAN

The U.S.A. went to war in Afghanistan after a terrorist attack on their country. On the morning of September 11th, 2001, two planes were **hijacked** and flown into the two towers of the World Trade Center in New York City, U.S.A.. These attacks, along with two other hijackings that took place in the U.S.A. on that day, killed nearly 3,000 people and are known as the September 11 attacks.

These attacks were planned by a **terrorist group** called al-Qaeda, who were based in Afghanistan. Their leader at the time, Osama bin Laden, was already wanted by the American government and after the attacks they decided that the group had to be stopped from causing more damage and loss of life.

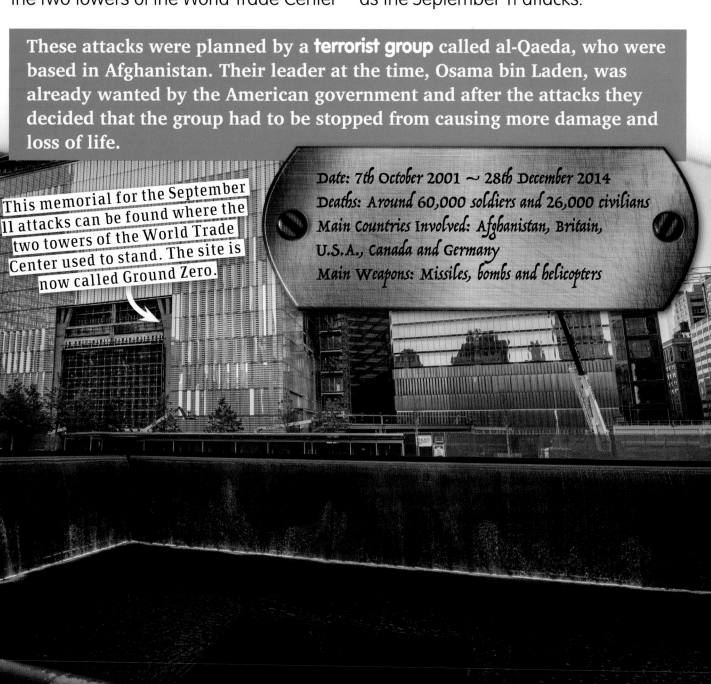

This memorial for the September 11 attacks can be found where the two towers of the World Trade Center used to stand. The site is now called Ground Zero.

Date: 7th October 2001 ~ 28th December 2014
Deaths: Around 60,000 soldiers and 26,000 civilians
Main Countries Involved: Afghanistan, Britain, U.S.A., Canada and Germany
Main Weapons: Missiles, bombs and helicopters

The majority of the fighting that took place in Afghanistan was guerrilla warfare. Soldiers moved around the country in small groups and both sides regularly used ambushes and bombs. American soldiers began to leave Afghanistan after Osama bin Laden was finally found and killed in 2011. By this time, he had avoided being found by America for over 10 years.

WORLD WARS

WORLD WAR I

When World War I (WWI) started in 1914, it quickly became the biggest and most complicated war that the world had ever seen.

The event that started the war was the **assassination** of the next king of **Austria-Hungary**, Archduke Franz Ferdinand, by a Serbian man named Gavrilo Princip. Believing that the Serbian government was behind the assassination, Austria-Hungary declared war on Serbia. After this, many of Serbia's and Austria-Hungary's allies joined the war.

Key:

- Allied Powers
- Central Powers
- Not involved

This map shows the countries that fought in WWI.

SERBIA AND THEIR ALLIES WERE CALLED THE ALLIED POWERS, WHEREAS AUSTRIA-HUNGARY AND THEIR ALLIES WERE CALLED THE CENTRAL POWERS.

TRENCH WARFARE

WWI is infamous for its trench warfare. Trench warfare is a type of conflict where deep trenches are dug into the ground in order to protect soldiers from enemy bullets and **artillery**. Both sides used trench warfare during WWI, which made it very easy to defend your own ground but very difficult to take new ground from the enemy. For much of the war, no side managed to take any ground from the other, but hundreds of thousands of soldiers died trying.

CHEMICAL WARFARE

The other major type of warfare used in WWI was chemical warfare, which had never been used in a war before. The trenches made it very difficult to attack the enemy using bullets or artillery, so both sides quickly started to use chemical warfare as it was able to reach the enemy in their trenches.

Date: 28th July 1914 ~ 11th November 1918
Deaths: Around 10 million soldiers and 7 million civilians
Main Allied Powers: France, Italy, Japan, Russia, Britain and the U.S.A.
Main Central Powers: Austria-Hungary, Bulgaria and Germany
Main Weapons: Machine guns, artillery and poison gas

A photograph taken of no man's land during WWI. No man's land is the space between two enemy trenches.

One of the worst chemicals used during WWI was chlorine gas, which burnt people's eyes, mouth, throat and lungs. Death from chlorine gas was very slow and painful and there was no way to treat it at the time. Soldiers on both sides usually had gas masks, however, these gas masks did not always work and they took a while to put on correctly. Because of this, huge clouds of chlorine gas were sent across no man's land in the hope that the enemy's gas masks would not be able to save them.

WORLD WAR II

World War II (WWII) was even larger, more deadly and more complicated than WWI. During the six years that WWII lasted, battles took place all over the world. WWII started when the Nazi Party in Germany, led by Adolf Hitler, invaded Poland in 1939.

THE GERMAN WORD FOR LIGHTNING IS 'BLITZ'. THE BOMBINGS IN BRITAIN WERE CALLED THE BLITZ BECAUSE THE BOMBS CAME FROM THE SKY AND CAUSED A LOT OF DAMAGE, JUST LIKE LIGHTNING.

Date: 1st September 1939 ~ 2nd September 1945
Deaths: Around 21 million soldiers and 50 million civilians
Main Allies: Britain, Soviet Union (Russia), France, U.S.A. and China
Main Axis Powers: Germany, Japan and Italy
Main Weapons: Tanks, machine guns and bombs

Warfare in WWII often involved bombs, which both sides used in order to attack civilians and destroy cities. Between September 1940 and May 1941, cities in Britain were bombed over 100 times in attacks known as the 'Blitz'. In these eight months, over 40,000 British civilians were killed by bombs in their own cities. Many parents moved their children to the countryside in order protect them from the bombs. These children, as well as other people who left the cities to escape the bombs, were called 'evacuees'. At night, people had to black-out their windows and turn off all of the lights so that enemy pilots flying over Britain couldn't see where the cities were.

WWII ended when the U.S.A. dropped a new kind of bomb, known as an atomic bomb, on two Japanese cities: Hiroshima and Nagasaki. The bombs were so powerful that these two bombings alone killed over 129,000 people, most of whom were civilians. Many people argue that the bombs should not have been dropped as they killed too many innocent people.

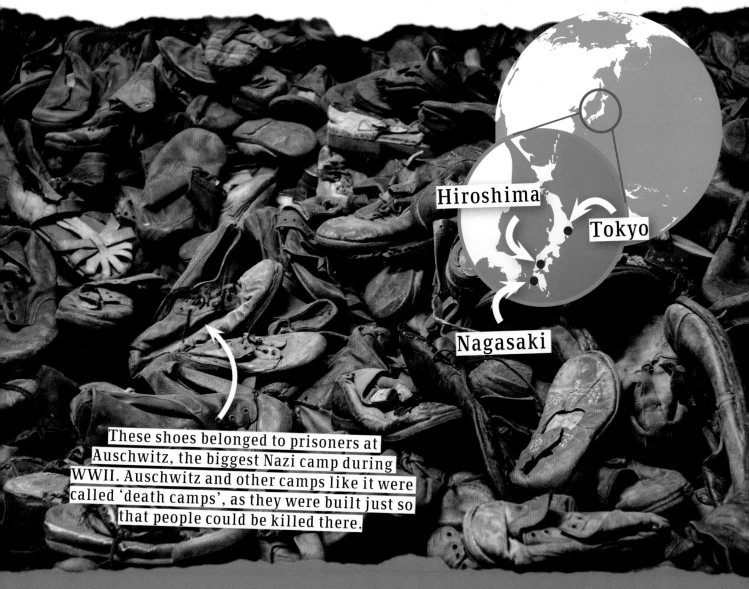

Hiroshima

Tokyo

Nagasaki

These shoes belonged to prisoners at Auschwitz, the biggest Nazi camp during WWII. Auschwitz and other camps like it were called 'death camps', as they were built just so that people could be killed there.

The most terrible event to occur during WWII was the Holocaust. The Holocaust was a genocide in which Adolf Hitler and his Nazi Party rounded-up and killed around six million Jewish people. The Nazis captured Jewish people in all of the countries that they invaded and sent them to camps. Here, they were either forced to do work in terrible conditions or were simply killed. Most of the people who died in these camps were killed by being sent into rooms that were then filled with poisonous gas. As well as this, another 5 million other people were killed for reasons such as being Polish, black, disabled or mentally ill. All of the people who died in the Holocaust were killed because Adolf Hitler believed that they were **inferior** types of people.

MORAL WARS

We understand that many terrible things happen in wars – people die, cities get destroyed and people lose their homes. Most people don't want these things to happen but accept that sometimes they have to occur in order to win a war. However, people often argue that there are some actions that can never be **justified**, even if they would win a war. These sorts of arguments are concerned with the morality of war.

A white flag is a symbol of surrender. Most people agree that it is immoral to attack someone who is waving a white flag.

ACTIONS THAT MOST PEOPLE BELIEVE TO BE RIGHT OR GOOD ARE SAID TO BE 'MORAL', WHEREAS ACTIONS THAT MOST PEOPLE BELIEVE TO BE WRONG OR BAD ARE SAID TO BE 'IMMORAL'.

The morality of an action is how right or wrong that action is. The morality of an action isn't just based on the action itself – it also looks at what happened before and what happened after the action was performed. For example, you can't just say that pushing your friends is always wrong, because sometimes it could be the right thing to do. Would it be wrong to push your friend out of the way of a car?

FORCE

A lot of people believe that it is immoral to use a large amount of force in a war. Here, 'force' means the number of soldiers, bullets and bombs that are used to complete a task – it is the amount of power used to attack an enemy.

Vietnam

NAPALM IS A SUBSTANCE THAT STICKS TO EVERYTHING IT TOUCHES. WHEN IT IS SET ON FIRE, IT IS TEN TIMES HOTTER THAN BOILING WATER.

Napalm bombs exploding in a field

Many people believe that the tactics used by American soldiers in the Vietnam War, which took place in Vietnam and other nearby countries between 1955 and 1975, were not moral because they used too much force. The Viet Cong, who were one of the groups that the Americans were fighting, fought the Americans using guerrilla warfare. Small groups of Viet Cong hid in villages in the jungles near to American bases and then waited to attack them. In order to attack the Viet Cong even when they were hiding, the Americans burnt down many villages and huge areas of jungle using napalm. Many people believe that these attacks were immoral as they used too much force and killed far more innocent people than Viet Cong soldiers.

CIVILIAN DEATH

Civilians are people who are not soldiers, who aren't helping their country to fight the war and who might not have wanted their country to go to war in the first place. These people are innocent and they have no part in the war. However, they can still get hurt by it.

Some people believe that every action that kills an innocent civilian is immoral. However, most people don't think it's that simple. If killing one innocent civilian would end a war that would otherwise kill thousands of soldiers, would it be worth it? Many people would say that it was worth it. But what if 100 civilians had to die? Or even 1,000 civilians?

This picture was taken just after the atomic bomb was dropped on Nagasaki on the 6th of August, 1945.

The atomic bombs that the U.S.A. dropped on the Japanese cities of Hiroshima and Nagasaki ended WWII, but they also killed 129,000 people. Most of these people were innocent civilians. While these bombs ended the war, many people think that it was immoral to drop the bombs as they killed too many innocent civilians.

LAST RESORT

The morality of a war doesn't only look at what happens during the war, it can also look at the reasons why the war started in the first place. Many people believe that the most immoral wars are the ones that were started for bad reasons. If the leader of one country went to war because they didn't like another country's flag, a lot of people would say that the war would always be immoral. This is because the war was started for a bad reason – soldiers would die, cities would be destroyed and money would be lost all because one person didn't like a flag.

Because of this, many people think that wars should always be a last resort. These people say that wars can only be moral when all other options have been tried first.

This might include talking with your enemy and trying to make peace with them. It can also mean thinking about surrendering to the enemy.

PEACE AND WAR TODAY

In many ways, the world has been getting more and more peaceful since the end of WWII. Fewer soldiers die in wars now than in any other period of history and the number of conflicts are decreasing in almost every part of the world.

However, as our technology has got better, the machines and weapons that are used in wars have become more powerful and deadly. Many armies around the world now have powerful artillery weapons, large air forces, many different types of bombs, strong **naval** forces, huge numbers of **landmines** and countless guns. These machines and weapons make the world a much more dangerous place for everyone, not just for the soldiers that are fighting in wars.

It is believed that there are over 60,000,000 landmines left in the ground from previous wars in Africa and Asia. On top of this, there are around 15,000 **nuclear weapons** in the world at the moment, many of which are more powerful than the bombs that were dropped on Japan at the end of WWII. While the world may be becoming more peaceful, it is still full of very powerful weapons.

ISRAEL AND PALESTINE

There are still many military conflicts going on around the world today. The longest-standing of these is the Israeli-Palestinian conflict that has been going on in the Middle East for over 50 years.

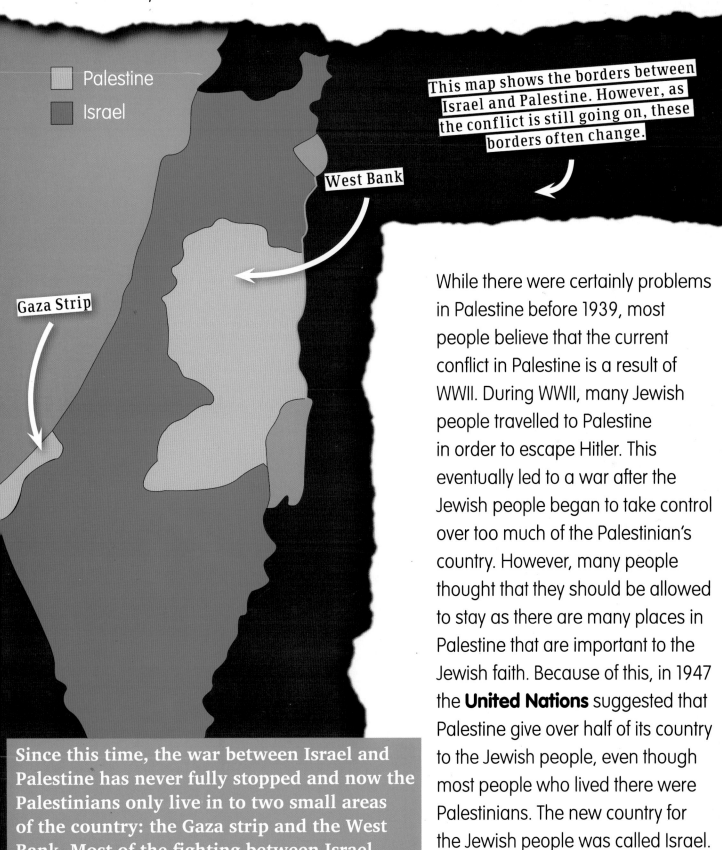

Palestine
Israel

West Bank

Gaza Strip

This map shows the borders between Israel and Palestine. However, as the conflict is still going on, these borders often change.

While there were certainly problems in Palestine before 1939, most people believe that the current conflict in Palestine is a result of WWII. During WWII, many Jewish people travelled to Palestine in order to escape Hitler. This eventually led to a war after the Jewish people began to take control over too much of the Palestinian's country. However, many people thought that they should be allowed to stay as there are many places in Palestine that are important to the Jewish faith. Because of this, in 1947 the **United Nations** suggested that Palestine give over half of its country to the Jewish people, even though most people who lived there were Palestinians. The new country for the Jewish people was called Israel.

Since this time, the war between Israel and Palestine has never fully stopped and now the Palestinians only live in to two small areas of the country: the Gaza strip and the West Bank. Most of the fighting between Israel and Palestine takes place in these two areas, making them dangerous places to live.

SYRIA

Syria is is currently one of the least peaceful countries on the planet and it has been at war for over five years.

The war began in 2011 as a civil war between the Syrian people and the Syrian government. The civil war meant that Syria was not being properly looked after by a government and this made it easier for other groups to join the fight. There were five major groups of people fighting in Syria in 2016, each of which had money and weapons sent to them by different countries around the world. Because so many other countries paid for the war, many people view the war in Syria as a proxy war.

This is the Arch of Triumph in Palmyra, Syria. It was built by the Romans over 1,500 years ago. In 2015, the Arch of Triumph was destroyed as a result of the war in Syria.

Syria

Since the start of the war, over half of the country's population has either been killed or forced to leave their homes. Over four million Syrians have become refugees, hundreds of thousands of soldiers and civilians have been killed and many important historical sites have been destroyed. This makes the Syrian Civil War the worst war of the 21st century.

Just because wars are still being fought around the world doesn't mean that world peace is not possible. While there are some countries, like Syria and Palestine, that have become less peaceful in the last few years, most countries around the world have become more peaceful. More children are now able to go to school. More people now have proper human rights. More people are tolerant of different cultures, religions and races. And more and more people now have the freedom to live their lives as they wish.

There are also lots of organisations around the world that help to keep places peaceful, improve human rights and make sure that people have the supplies and resources that they need to survive.

If we all continue to be tolerant of peoples' differences, support everyone's right to be free and give money to the organisations that help people, then world peace might not be too far away.

CLASS DISCUSSIONS

What do you think is the worst consequence of war? Discuss your thoughts with other people in your class.

In your opinion, what is most important when trying to ensure that a war is moral?

Not using too much force.

Making sure that civilians are not hurt.

Making sure that it is a last resort.

Think about the different reasons why countries might go to war. Can you think of any situation where going to war would be the right thing to do?

GLOSSARY

allies	countries that work together, often for military reasons
ammunition	bullets, shells, missiles and bombs
artillery	very large guns used in warfare on land
assassination	the killing of an important person, usually for political or religious reasons
atrocity	an extremely cruel act
Austria-Hungary	an empire made up of the lands owned by Austria and Hungary that existed from 1867 to 1918
civilians	people not in the army or police force
colonies	areas under the control of another country and occupied by people from that country
conflict	a serious disagreement or fight
consequences	the results or effects of an action or actions
culture	the traditions, ideas and ways of life of a particular group of people
governments	groups of people with the authority to run countries and decide their laws
hijacked	to have taken control of a vehicle illegally
human rights	rights that every person should have
humane	showing kindness and a respect for life
independent	free from outside control
inferior	worse in quality or lower in status
issues	important topics or problems
justified	done for a good reason
landmines	bombs laid on or just under the ground
memorial	a statue or structure that is meant to remind people about a certain person or event
military	a country's army and the things that relate to it
naval	relating to a navy, which is the part of an army that operates at sea
nuclear weapons	very destructive weapons that use nuclear energy
race	a group of people who have similar characteristics and share the same culture and history
surrendered	stopped fighting the enemy and accepted that the enemy had won
tactics	carefully planned actions and strategies in a war
taxes	payments made to the government so that they can provide services
terrain	the physical features of a stretch of land
terrorist group	people who cause damage and death in order to scare and intimidate governments and civilians
tolerant	able to accept beliefs, opinions and behaviours that you disagree with
tranquillity	the state of being calm and free from disturbance
United Nations	an international organisation created in 1945 to promote peace and cooperation between countries
values	standards of behaviour and beliefs on what is important in life

INDEX